EASY
SPANISH
PHRASE BOOK
Over 770 Basic Phrases
for Everyday Use

DOVER PUBLICATIONS, INC.
NEW YORK

Bibliographical Note

The material in this book was originally published by Dover in 1959 as part of a manual to accompany a recording entitled *Listen & Learn Spanish*. The English outline was prepared by the editorial staff of Dover Publications, Inc. The Spanish translation and transliteration were prepared by Frank Thompson.

Library of Congress Cataloging-in-Publication Data

Easy Spanish phrase book : over 770 basic phrases for everyday use.
    p.   cm.
  ISBN 0-486-28086-1 (pbk.)
  1. Spanish language—Conversation and phrase books—English.   I. Dover Publications, Inc.
PC4121.E38 1994
468.3'421—dc20   94–15611
                                                                                CIP

Manufactured in the United States of America
Dover Publications, Inc., 31 East 2nd Street, Mineola, N.Y. 11501

CONTENTS

INTRODUCTION

This book is designed to teach you the basic words, phrases and sentences that you will need for simple everyday communication wherever Spanish is spoken.* It does not attempt to teach you the grammatical structure of Spanish, but instead helps you to express your needs and handle problems encountered while traveling.

The value of the book rests as much on what is omitted as on what is included. An effort has been made to include only those phrases pertinent to the needs of the traveler. You will find the phrase "I want small change" (a frequent need in travel), but do not expect to find a sentence like "This is the pen of my aunt." Furthermore, since the material presented here is not cumulative, as it is in conventional foreign-language courses, you need not start at the beginning. Study whichever phrases will be the most useful to you.

The focus of instruction is on what *you* will say. However, the section entitled "Making Yourself Understood," which contains such vital phrases as "Please speak more slowly" and "Repeat it, please," will aid you in understanding others.

This book is complete in itself and is meant to be used for reference and study. Read it at odd moments and try to learn ten or fifteen phrases a day. Also, be sure to take the manual with you when you go abroad. All that you have learned will be available for reference and review.

The book is designed to help you form additional Spanish sentences from the sentences it provides. You can do this by substituting a new word for a given word in a familiar sentence. In sentences where this is possible, the candidate for substitution appears in brackets, and is sometimes followed by possible alternatives. For example,

> I am [a student]
> —teacher
> —businessman

provides three sentences: "I am a student," "I am a teacher" and "I am a businessman."

---

*The grammar, pronunciation and vocabulary represent Latin American usage. However, you will be understood without difficulty in all Spanish-speaking countries.

Another especially helpful feature is the extensive topic and word index beginning on page 62. Notice that each entry in the book is numbered and that the index refers to these numbers. This enables you to locate information you need quickly, without having to search the entire page.

SPANISH PRONUNCIATION

This book uses a phonetic transcription as an aid to correct pronunciation. (See "Scheme of Pronunciation," below.) It usually appears below the Spanish line in the text.

SCHEME OF PRONUNCIATION

Letter	Tran-scription	Example	Notes
a	ah	as in *father*, but cut short	
b	b	as in *boy*	
c	s OR k	as in *say* or *skin*	*c* is pronounced like *s* before *e* and *i*; like *k* before all other vowels and consonants.
ch	ch	as in *church*	
d	d	as in *day*	
e	e OR ay	as in *met* or in *day*, but cut short	
f	f	as in *fall*	
g	g OR h	as in *go* or *hold*	*g* is pronounced like *h* before *e* and *i*; before all other vowels and consonants it is hard, as in *go*.

Letter	Tran-scription	Example	Notes
h	—	silent	
i	ee	as in feel, but cut short	
j	h	as in hold	
l	l	as in let	
ll	y	as in yes	
m	m	as in met	
n	n	as in not	
ñ	ny	as in canyon	
o	o OR oh	as in note, but cut short	
p	p	as in spin	
q	k	as in skin	
r	r	as in red	Tap the r with the tip of the tongue.
rr	rr	as in red	More strongly trilled than a single r.
s	s	as in say	
t	t	as in sting	
u	oo	as in food, but cut short	
v	v	as in vase	
x	ks	as in picks	
y	ee	as in feel, but cut short	
z	s	as in say	

NOTE: *hay* has been transcribed as *I* in "I am" and *ai* has been transcribed as *ie* in "lie".

GREETINGS, INTRODUCTIONS AND SOCIAL CONVERSATION

1. Good morning.
Buenos días.
BWAY-nohss DEE-ahss.

2. Good evening.
Buenas noches.
BWAY-nahss NO-chess.

3. Goodbye.
Adiós.
ah-DYOHSS.

4. Until next time.
Hasta la vista.
AHSS-tah lah VEESS-tah.

5. I wish to make an appointment with [Mr. Gonzáles].
Quiero hacer una cita con [el señor González].
KYAY-ro ah-SAYR OO-nah SEE-tah kohn [el say-NYOR gohn-SAH-less].

6. May I introduce [Mr., Mrs., Miss Garcia].
Permítame presentar [al señor, a la señora, a la señorita Garcia].
payr-MEE-tah-may pray-sen-TAHR [ahl say-NYOR, ah lah say-NYOH-rah, ah la say-nyoh-REE-tah gar-SEE-ah].

7. —— my wife.
mi esposa.
mee ess-PO-sah.

8. —— my husband.
mi esposo.
mee ess-PO-so.

9. —— my daughter.
mi hija.
mee EE-hah.

10. —— my son.
mi hijo.
mee EE-ho.

11. —— my friend.
mi amigo (*masc.*).
mee ah-MEE-go.

12. —— my sister.
mi hermana.
mee ayr-MAH-nah.

13. —— my brother.
mi hermano.
mee ayr-MAH-no.

14. —— my mother.
mi madre.
mee MAH-dray.

15. —— my father.
mi padre.
mee PAH-dray.

16. —— my child.
mi hijo (*masc.*).
mee EE-ho.

17. I am glad to meet you.
Me alegro de conocerle.
may ah-LAY-gro day ko-no-SAYR-lay.

18. How are you?
¿Cómo está usted?
KO-mo ess-TAH oos-TED?

19. Fine, thanks.   And you?
Muy bien, gracias.   ¿Y usted?
mwee byen, GRAH-syahss.   ee oos-TED?

20. How are things?
¿Qué tal?
kay tahl?

21. All right.
Bien.
byen.

22. So, so.
Así, así.
ah-SEE, ah-SEE.

23. How is your family?
¿Cómo está su familia?
KO-mo ess-TAH soo fah-MEE-lyah?

24. Very well.
Muy bien.
mwee byen.

25. Please sit down.
Haga el favor de sentarse.
AH-gah el fah-VOR day sen-TAHR-say.

26. I have enjoyed myself very much.
Me he divertido mucho.
may ay dee-vayr-TEE-doh MOO-cho.

27. Give my regards to your aunt and uncle.
Dé mis recuerdos a sus tíos.
day meess ray-KWAYR-dohss ah sooss TEE-ohss.

28. Come to see us.
Venga a vernos.
VEN-gah ah VAYR-nohss.

29. Give me your address and telephone number.
Déme su dirección y su número de teléfono.
DAY may soo dee-rek-SYOHN ee soo NOO-may-roh day tay-LAY-fo-no.

30. May I call on you again?
¿Me permite visitarle otra vez?
may payr-MEE-tay vee-see-TAHR-lay O-trah vess?

31. I like you very much.
Me simpatiza mucho.
may seem-pah-TEE-sah MOO-cho.

32. Congratulations.
Felicitaciones.
fay-lee-see-tah-SYOH-ness.

33. Happy birthday.
Feliz cumpleaños.
fay-LEESS coom-play-AHN-yohss.

34. Happy New Year.
Feliz año nuevo.
fay-LEESS AHN-yo NWAY-vo.

35. Merry Christmas.
Feliz Navidad.
fay-LEESS nah-vee-DAHD.

YOURSELF

36. My name is [John].
Me llamo [Juan].
may YAH-mo [hwahn].

37. I am an American citizen.
Soy ciudadano americano.
soy syoo-dah-DAH-no ah-may-ree-KAH-no.

38. My mailing address is 920 Broadway.
Mi dirección para cartas es novecientos veinte Broadway.
mee dee-rek-SYOHN PAH-rah KAHR-tahss ess no-vay-SYEN-tohss VAYN-tay Broadway.

39. I am a [student].
Soy [estudiante].
soy [ess-too-DYAHN-tay].

40. —— teacher.
profesor (*masc.*).
pro-feh-SSOR.

41. —— businessman.
hombre de negocios.
OHM-bray day nay-GO-ssyohs.

42. I am a friend of Robert's.
Soy un amigo de Roberto.
soy oon ah-MEE-go day ro-BAYR-toh.

43. I am here on [a business trip] a vacation.
Estoy aquí [de negocios] de vacaciones.
ess-TOY ah-KEE [day nay-GO-see-ohss] day vah-kah-SYOH-ness.

44. We are traveling to Barcelona.
Viajamos a Barcelona.
vyah-HAH-mohss ah bahr-say-LO-nah.

45. I am in a hurry.
Tengo prisa.
TEN-go PREE-sah.

46. I am [hungry] thirsty.
Tengo [hambre] sed.
TEN-go [AHM-bray] sed.

47. I am [warm] cold.
Tengo [calor] frío.
TEN-go [kah-LOHR] FREE-o.

48. I am glad.
Me alegro.
may ah-LAY-gro.

49. I am sorry.
Lo siento.
lo SYEN-toh.

MAKING YOURSELF UNDERSTOOD

50. Do you speak English?
¿Habla usted inglés?
AH-blah oos-TED een-GLAYSS?

51. Does anyone here speak English?
¿Hay alguien aquí que hable inglés?
I AHL-gyen ah-KEE kay AH-blay een-GLAYSS?

52. I speak only English.
Sólo hablo inglés.
SO-lo AH-blo een-GLAYSS.

53. I speak a little Spanish.
Hablo un poco de español.
AH-blo oon PO-ko day ess-pah-NYOHL.

54. Please speak more slowly.
Favor de hablar más despacio.
fah-VOR day ah-BLAHR mahss day-PAH-syoh.

55. I (do not) understand.
(No) comprendo.
(no) kohm-PREN-doh.

56. Do you understand me?
¿Me comprende?
may kohm-PREN-day?

57. I (do not) know.
(No) se.
(no) say.

58. I think so.
Creo que sí.
KRAY-oh kay see.

59. Repeat it, please.
Favor de repetirlo.
fah-VOR day rray-pay-TEER-lo.

60. Write it down, please.
Escríbalo, por favor.
ess-KREE-bah-lo, por fah-VOR.

61. What does this word mean?
¿Qué quiere decir esta palabra?
kay KYAY-ray day-SEER ESS-tah pah-LAH-brah?

62. What is that?
¿Qué es eso?
kay ess AY-so?

63. How do you say "match" in Spanish?
¿Cómo se dice "match" en español?
KO-mo say DEE-say "match" en ess-pah-NYOHL?

USEFUL WORDS AND EXPRESSIONS

64. Yes.
Sí.
see.

65. No.
No.
no.

66. Perhaps.
Puede ser.
PWAY-day sayr.

67. Excuse me.
Dispénseme.
deess-PEN-say-may.

68. Thanks (very much).
(Muchas) gracias.
(MOO-chahss) GRAH-syahss.

69. You are welcome.
No hay de que.
no I day kay.

70. It is all right.
Está bien.
ess-TAH byen.

71. It doesn't matter.
No importa.
no eem-POR-tah.

72. That is all.
Eso es todo.
AY-so ess TOH-doh.

73. Who are you?
¿Quién es usted?
kyen ess oos-TED?

74. Who is [that boy]?
¿Quién es [ese muchacho]?
kyen ess [ESS-ay moo-CHAH-cho]?

75. —— that girl.
esa muchacha.
ESS-ah moo-CHAH-chah.

76. —— **that man.**
ese hombre.
ESS-ay OHM-bray.

77. —— **that woman.**
esa mujer.
ESS-ah moo-HAYR.

78. Where is [the men's room]?
¿Dónde está [el cuarto de caballeros]?
DOHN-day ess-TAH [el KWAR-toh day kah-bah-YAY-rohss]?

79. —— **the ladies' room.**
el cuarto de damas.
el KWAR-toh day DAH-mahss.

80. Who?
¿Quién?
kyen?

81. What?
¿Qué?
kay?

82. Why?
¿Por qué?
por kay?

83. When?
¿Cuándo?
KWAHN-doh?

84. Where?
¿Dónde?
DOHN-day?

85. How?
¿Cómo?
KO-mo?

86. How much?
¿Cuánto?
KWAHN-toh?

87. How long?
¿Cuánto tiempo?
KWAHN-toh TYEM-po?

88. What do you wish?
¿Qué desea usted?
kay day-SAY-ah oos-TED?

89. Come here.
Venga acá.
VEN-gah ah-KAH.

90. Come in.
Pase usted.
PAH-say oos-TED.

91. Wait a moment.
Espere un momento.
ess-PAY-ray oon mo-MEN-toh.

92. Listen.
Oiga.
OY-gah.

93. Look out!
¡Cuidado!
kwee-DAH-doh!

DIFFICULTIES

94. Can you [help me] tell me?
¿Puede usted [ayudarme] decirme?
PWAY-day oos-TED [ah-yoo-DAHR-may] day- SEER-may?

95. I am looking for my friends.
Busco a mis amigos.
BOOS-ko ah meess ah-MEE-gohss.

96. I cannot find my hotel address.
No puedo hallar la dirección de mi hotel.
no PWAY-doh ah-YAHR lah dee-rek-SYOHN day mee o-TEL.

97. I lost [my purse] my wallet.
No encuentro [mi bolsa] mi cartera.
no en-KWEN-tro [mee BOHL-sah] mee kahr-TAY-rah.

98. I forgot my money.
Olvidé mi dinero.
ohl-vee-DAY mee dee-NAY-ro.

99. I have missed my train.
He perdido mi tren.
ay payr-DEE-doh mee tren.

100. What am I to do?
¿Qué debo hacer?
kay DAY-bo ah-SAYR?

101. My eyeglasses are broken.
Mis gafas están rotas.
meess GAH-fahs ess-TAHN RO-tahss.

102. Can you repair these shoes?
¿Puede componerme estos zapatos?
PWAY-day kom-po-NAYR-may ESS-tohs sah-PAH-tohss?

103. The lost - and - found desk.
La sección de objetos perdidos.
lah sek-SYOHN day ohb-HAY-tohss payr-DEE-dohss.

104. The police station.
La estación de policía.
lah ess-tah-SYOHN day po-lee-SEE-ah.

105. I will call a policeman.
Llamaré un policía.
yah-mah-RAY oon po-lee-SEE-ah.

106. The American consulate.
El consulado americano.
el kohn-soo-LAH-doh ah-may-ree-KAH-no.

CUSTOMS

107. Where is the customs?
¿Dónde está la aduana?
DOHN-day ess-TAH lah ah-DWAH-nah?

108. Here is [my baggage].
Aquí está [mi equipaje].
ah-KEE ess-TAH [mee ay-kee-PAH-hay].

109. —— my passport.
    mi pasaporte.
    mee pah-sah-POR-tay.

110. —— my identification papers.
    mi carnet de identificación.
    mee kahr-NAY day ee-den-tee-fee-kah-SYOHN.

111. —— my health certificate.
    mi certificado de salud.
    mee sayr-tee-fee-KAH-doh day sah-LOOD.

112. The bags to your left are mine.
Las maletas a su izquierda son las mías.
lahs mah-LAY-tahss ah soo eess-KYAYR-dah sohn lahs MEE-ahs.

113. I have nothing to declare.
No tengo nada que declarar.
no TEN-go NAH-dah kay day-klah-RAHR.

114. All this is for my personal use.
Todo esto es para mi uso personal.
TOH-doh ESS-toh ess PAH-rah mee OO-so payr-so-NAHL.

115. Must I open everything?
¿Tengo que abrir todo?
TEN-go kay ah-BREER TOH-doh?

116. There is nothing here but clothing.
No hay más que ropa aquí.
no I mahss kay RROH-pah ah-KEE.

117. These are gifts.
Estos son regalos.
ESS-tohss sohn rray-GAH-lohss.

118. Are these things dutiable?
¿Hay que pagar impuestos sobre estos artículos?
I kay pah-GAHR eem-PWESS-tohss SO-bray ESS-tohss ahr-TEE-koo-lohss?

119. How much must I pay?
¿Cuánto tengo que pagar?
KWAHN-toh TEN-go kay pah-GAHR?

120. This is all I have.
Esto es todo lo que tengo.
ESS-toh ess TOH-doh lo kay TEN-go.

121. Have you finished?
¿Ha terminado usted?
ah tayr-mee-NAH-doh oos-TED?

BAGGAGE

122. Where can I check my baggage through to Buenos Aires?
¿Dónde puedo hacer enviar mi equipaje a Buenos Aires?
DOHN-day PWAY-doh ah-SER en-VYAHR mee ay-kee-PAH-hay ah BWAY-nohss I-rayss?

123. The baggage room.
La sala de equipajes.
lah SAH-lah day ay-kee-PAH-hess.

124. I want to leave these packages for a while.
Quiero dejar estos paquetes un rato.
KYAY-ro day-HAHR ESS-tohss pah-KAY-tess oon RRAH-toh.

125. Handle this very carefully.
Mucho cuidado con esto.
MOO-cho kwee-DAH-doh kohn ESS-toh.

126. Put everything in a taxi.
Ponga todo en un taxi.
POHN-gah TOH-doh en oon TAHK-see.

TRAVEL: GENERAL EXPRESSIONS

127. I want to go [to the airline office].
Quiero ir [a la oficina de la línea aérea].
KYAY-ro eer [ah lah o-fee-SEE-nah day lah LEE-nay-ah ah-AY-ray-ah].

128. —— to the travel agent's office.
a la oficina del agente de viajes.
ah lah o-fee-SEE-nah del ah-HEN-tay day VYAH-hays.

129. How long does it take to go to Madrid?
¿En cuánto tiempo se llega a Madrid?
en KWAHN-toh TYEM-po say YAY-gah ah mah-DREED?

130. When will we arrive at Barcelona?
¿Cuándo llegaremos a Barcelona?
KWAHN-doh yay-gah-RAY-mohss ah bahr-say-LO-nah?

131. Is this the direct way to the Prado?
¿Es éste el camino directo al Prado?
ess ESS-tay el kah-MEE-no dee-REK-toh ahl PRAH-doh?

132. Please show me the way [to the business section].
Por favor dígame cómo se llega [al centro].
por fah-VOR DEE-gah-may KO-mo say YAY-gah [ahl SEN-tro].

133. —— to the residential section.
a la sección residencial.
ah lah sek-SYOHN ray-see-den-SYAHL.

134. —— to the city.
a la ciudad.
ah lah syoo-DAHD.

135. —— to the village.
al pueblo.
ahl PWAY-blo.

136. Where do I turn?
¿Dónde doy vuelta?
DOHN-day doy VWELL-tah?

137. —— **to the north.**
al norte.
ahl NOR-tay.

138. —— **to the south.**
al sur.
ahl soor.

139. —— **to the east.**
al este.
ahl ESS-tay.

140. —— **to the west.**
al oeste.
ahl o-ESS-tay.

141. —— **to the right.**
a la derecha.
ah lah day-RAY-chah.

142. —— **to the left.**
a la izquierda.
ah lah eess-KYAYR-dah.

143. —— **at the traffic light.**
dónde está el semáforo.
DOHN-day ess-TAH el say-MAH-fo-ro.

144. Where is it?
¿Dónde está?
DOHN-day ess-TAH?

145. This way.
Por aquí.
por ah-KEE.

146. That way.
Por allí.
por ah-YEE.

147. Is it [on this side of the street]?
¿Está [de este lado de la calle]?
ess-TAH [day ESS-tay LAH-doh day lah KAH-yay]?

148. —— **on the other side of the street.**
del otro lado de la calle.
del O-tro LAH-doh day lah KAH-yay.

149. —— **at the corner.**
en la esquina.
en lah ess-KEE-nah.

150. —— **in the middle.**
en medio.
en MAY-dyoh.

151. —— **straight ahead.**
adelante.
ah-day-LAHN-tay.

152. —— **opposite the park.**
frente al parque.
FREN-tay ahl PAHR-kay.

153. —— **behind the school.**
detrás de la escuela.
day-TRAHSS day lah ess-KWAY-lah.

154. —— **in front of the monument.**
frente al monumento.
FREN-tay ahl mo-noo-MAYN-toh.

155. —— **forward.**
adelante.
ah-day-LAHN-tay.

156. —— **back.**
atrás.
ah-TRAHSS.

157. How far is it?
¿A qué distancia está?
ah kay deess-TAHN-syah ess-TAH?

158. Can I walk there?
¿Puedo llegar a pie?
PWAY-doh yay-GAHR ah pyay?

159. Am I going in the right direction?
¿Voy bien?
voy byen?

160. What street is this?
¿Qué calle es ésta?
kay KAH-yay ess ESS-tah?

TICKETS

161. Where is the ticket office?
¿Dónde está la taquilla?
DOHN-day ess-TAH lah tah-KEE-yah?

162. How much is [a round-trip ticket] to Caracas?
¿Cuánto cuesta [un billete de ida y vuelta] a Caracas?
KWAHN-toh KWESS-tah [oon bee-YAY-tay day EE-dah ee VWELL-tah] ah kah-RAH-kahss?

163. —— a one-way ticket.
un billete sencillo.
oon bee-YAY-tay sen-SEE-yo.

164. First class.
Primera clase.
pree-MAY-rah KLAH-say.

165. Second class.
Segunda clase.
say-GOON-dah KLAH-say.

166. Third class.
Tercera clase.
tayr-SAY-rah KLAH-say.

167. Local.
Local.
lo-KAHL.

168. Express.
Rápido.
RAH-pee-doh.

169. A reserved seat.
Un asiento apartado.
oon ah-SYEN-toh ah-pahr-TAH-doh.

170. The waiting room.
La sala de espera.
lah SAH-lah day ess-PAY-rah.

171. May I stop at Seville on the way?
¿Puedo parar en Sevilla en camino?
PWAY-doh pah-RAHR en say-VEE-yah en kah-MEE-no?

BOAT

172. When must I go on board?
¿A qué hora debo estar a bordo?
ah kay O-rah DAY-bo ess-TAHR ah BOHR-doh?

173. Bon voyage.
Buen viaje.
bwen VYAH-hay.

174. The captain.
El capitán.
el kah-pee-TAHN.

175. The purser.
El contador.
el kohn-tah-DOR.

176. The steward.
El camarero.
el kah-mah-RAY-ro.

177. The cabin.
El camarote.
el kah-mah-RO-tay.

178. The deck.
La cubierta.
lah koo-BYAYR-tah.

179. The lifeboat.
La lancha.
lah LAHN-chah.

180. The dock.
El muelle.
el MWAY-yay.

181. The life preserver.
El salvavidas.
el sahl-vah-VEE-dahss.

182. I feel seasick.
Estoy mareado.
ess-TOY mah-ray-AH-doh.

AIRPLANE

183. Is there bus service to the airport?
¿Hay servicio de transporte al aeropuerto?
I sayr-VEE-syoh day trahnss-POR-tay ahl ah-ay-ro-PWAYR-toh?

184. At what time will they come for me?
¿A qué hora vienen por mí?
ah kay O-rah VYAY-nen por mee?

185. Is flight 23 on time?
¿Está a tiempo el vuelo veintitrés?
ess-TAH ah TYEM-po el VWAY-lo vayn-tee-TRAYSS?

186. How many kilos may I take?
¿Cuántos kilos puedo llevar?
KWAHN-tohss KEE-lohss PWAY-doh yay-VAHR?

187. How much per kilo for excess?
¿Cuánto por kilo de exceso?
KWAHN-toh por KEE-lo day ek-SAY-so?

TRAIN

188. Where is the railroad station?
¿Dónde está la estación de ferrocarriles?
DOHN-day ess-TAH lah ess-tah-SYOHN day fay- rro-kah-RREE-less?

189. When does the train for Oaxaca leave?
¿Cuándo sale el tren para Oaxaca?
KWAHN-doh SAH-lay el tren PAH-rah wah-HAH- kah?

190. The arrival.
La llegada.
lah yay-GAH-dah.

191. The departure.
La salida.
lah sah-LEE-dah.

192. From what track does the train leave?
¿De cuál andén sale el tren?
day kwahl ahn-DAYN SAH-lay el trayn?

193. Please [open the window].
Favor de [abrir la ventanilla].
fah-VOR day [ah-BREER lah ven-tah-NEE-yah].

194. —— close the window.
cerrar la ventanilla.
say-RRAHR lah ven-tah-NEE-yah.

195. Where is [the diner].
¿Dónde está [el comedor]?
DOHN-day ess-TAH [el ko-may-DOR]?

196. ——the sleeper.
el coche-cama.
el KOH-chay-KAH-mah.

197. Where is the smoking car?
¿Dónde queda el coche fumador?
DOHN-day KAY-dah el KOH-chay foo-mah-DOHR?

198. May I smoke?
¿Se puede fumar?
say PWAY-day foo-MAHR?

BUS AND STREETCAR

199. What streetcar do I take to the plaza?
¿Qué tranvía tomo para la plaza?
kay trahn-VEE-ah TOH-mo PAH-rah lah PLAH- sah?

200. The bus stop.
La parada.
lah pah-RAH-dah.

201. A transfer.
Un transbordo.
oon trahnss-BOR-doh.

202. Where does the streetcar for the main street stop?
¿Dónde para el tranvía que va a la calle principal?
DOHN-day PAH-rah el trahn-VEE-ah kay vah ah lah KAH-yay preen-see-PAHL?

203. Does the bus stop at the avenue?
¿Para este autobús en la avenida?
PAH-rah ESS-tay ow-toh-BOOSS en lah ah-vay-NEE-dah?

204. Do you go near the circle?
¿Pasa usted por la rotonda?
PAH-sah oos-TED por lah ro-TOHN-dah?

205. Do I have to change?
¿Tengo que cambiar?
TEN-go kay kahm-BYAHR?

206. Driver, please tell me where to get off.
Conductor, por favor, avíseme dónde me bajo.
kohn-dook-TOHR, por fah-VOR, ah-VEE-say-may DOHN-day may BAH-ho.

207. I want to get off at the next stop.
Quiero bajarme en la próxima parada.
KYAY-ro bah-HAHR-may en lah PROHK-see-mah pah-RAH-dah.

TAXI

208. Please call a taxi for me.
Haga el favor de llamarme un taxi.
AH-gah el fah-VOR day yah-MAHR-may oon TAHK-see.

209. Are you free?
¿Está libre?
ess-TAH LEE-bray?

210. What do you charge [per hour]?
¿Cuánto cobra [por hora]?
KWAHN-toh KO-brah [por O rah]?

211. —— per kilometer.
por kilómetro.
por kee-LO-may-troh.

212. Please drive [more slowly].
Por favor, conduzca [más despacio].
por fah-VOR, kohn-DOOSS-kah [mahss dess-PAH- syoh].

213. —— more carefully.
con más cuidado.
kohn mahss kwee-DAH-doh.

214. Stop here.
Pare aquí.
PAH-ray ah-KEE.

215. Wait for me.
Espéreme.
ess-PAY-ray-may.

AUTOMOBILE TRAVEL

216. Where can I rent a car?
¿Dónde puedo alquilar un auto?
DOHN-day PWAY-doh ahl-kee-LAHR oon OW-toh?

217. I have an international driver's license.
Tengo una licencia internacional.
TEN-go OO-nah lee-SEN-syah een-tayr-nah-syoh-NAHL.

218. A gas station.
Un expendio de gasolina.
oon es-PEN-dyoh day gah-so-LEE-nah.

219. A garage.
Un garaje.
oon gah-RAH-hay.

220. A mechanic.
Un mecánico.
oon may-KAH-nee-ko.

221. Is the road [good] bad?
¿Está el camino en [buenas] malas condiciones?
ess-TAH el kah-MEE-no en [BWAY-nahss] MAH- lahss kohn-dee-SYOH-ness?

222. Where does that road go?
¿Adónde conduce aquel camino?
ah-DOHN-day kohn-DOO-say ah-KEL kah-MEE-no?

223. What town is this?
¿Cómo se llama este pueblo?
KO-mo say YAH-mah ESS-tay PWAY-blo?

224. The next one?
¿El próximo?
el PROHK-see-mo?

225. Can you show me on the map?
¿Puede indicarme en el mapa?
PWAY-day een-dee-KAHR-may en el MAH-pah?

226. How much is gas a liter?
¿Cuánto cuesta la gasolina por litro?
KWAHN-toh KWESS-tah lah gah-so-LEE-nah por LEE-troh?

227. The tank is [empty] full.
El tanque está [vacío] lleno.
el TAHN-kay ess-TAH [vah-SEE-o] YAY-no.

228. Give me forty liters.
Déme cuarenta litros.
DAY-may kwah-REN-tah LEE-trohss.

229. Please change the oil.
Por favor, cambie el aceite.
por fah-VOR, KAHM-byay el ah-SAY-tay.

230. Put water in the battery.
Ponga agua en el acumulador.
POHN-gah AH-gwah en el ah-koo-moo-lah-DOR.

231. Will you lubricate the car?
¿Quiere engrasar el coche?
KYAY-ray en-grah-SAHR el KO-chay?

232. Adjust the brakes.
Ajuste los frenos.
ah-HOOSS-tay lohss FRAY-nohss.

233. Will you check the tires?
¿Quiere usted revisar las llantas?
KYAY-ray oos-TED rray-vee-SAHR lahss YAHN-tahss?

234. Can you fix [the flat tire] now?
¿Puede componerme [la llanta] ahora?
PWAY-day kohm-po-NAYR-may [lah YAHN-tah] ah-O-rah?

235. —— **a puncture.**
un pinchazo.
oon peen-CHAH-so.

236. —— **a slow leak.**
un escape.
oon ess-KAH-pay.

237. The engine overheats.
El motor se calienta.
el mo-TOHR say kah-LYEN-tah.

238. The motor [misses] stalls.
El motor [falla] se para.
el mo-TOHR [FAH-yah] say PAH-rah.

239. May I park here for a while?
¿Me permite estacionarme aquí un rato?
may payr-MEE-tay ess-tah-syoh-NAHR-may ah-KEE oon RRAH-toh?

AT THE HOTEL

240. I am looking for [a good hotel].
Busco [un buen hotel].
BOOS-ko [oon bwayn o-TEL].

241. —— **an inexpensive hotel.**
un hotel barato.
oon o-TEL bah-RAH-toh.

242. —— **a boarding house.**
una casa de huéspedes.
OO-nah KAH-sah day WESS-pay-dayss.

243. —— **a furnished apartment.**
un apartamiento amueblado.
oon ah-pahr-tah-MYEN-toh ah-mway-BLAH- doh.

244. I (do not) want to be in the center of town.
(No) quiero estar en el centro.
(no) KYAY-ro ess-TAHR en el SEN-tro.

245. Where it is not noisy.
Dónde no haya ruido.
DOHN-day no AH-yah RRWEE-doh.

20

246. I have a reservation for today.
Tengo reservado para hoy.
TEN-go rray-sayr-VAH-doh PAH-rah oy.

247. Do you have [a vacancy]?
¿Tiene [cuarto]?
TYAY-nay [KWAHR-toh]?

248. —— an air-conditioned room.
un cuarto con aire acondicionado.
oon KWAHR-toh kohn I-ray ah-kohn-dee-syoh- NAH-doh.

249. —— a single room.
un cuarto para uno.
oon KWAHR-toh PAH-rah OO-no.

250. —— a double room.
un cuarto para dos.
oon KWAHR-toh PAH-rah dohss.

251. I want a room [for tonight].
Quiero un cuarto [para esta noche].
KYAY-ro oon KWAHR-toh [PAH-rah ESS-tah No-chay].

252. —— for two persons.
para dos personas.
PAH-rah dohss payr-SOH-nahss.

253. —— with a double bed.
con cama matrimonial.
kohn KAH-mah mah-tree-mo-NYAHL.

254. —— with twin beds.
con camas gemelas.
kohn KAH-mahss hay-MAY-lahss.

255. —— with a bath.
con baño.
kohn BAH-nyoh.

256. —— with a shower.
con ducha.
kohn DOO-chah.

257. —— with a sink.
con lavabo.
kohn lah-VAH-bo.

258. —— with a balcony.
con balcón.
kohn bahl-KOHN.

259. —— **without meals.**
sin comidas.
seen koh-MEE-dahs.

260. What is the rate per day?
¿Cuánto cuesta por día?
KWAHN-toh KWESS-tah por DEE-ah?

261. I should like to see the room.
Quisiera ver el cuarto.
kee-SYAY-rah vayr el KWAHR-toh.

262. Is it [upstairs] downstairs?
¿Está [arriba] abajo?
ess-TAH [ah-RREE-bah] ah-BAH-ho?

263. Is there an elevator?
¿Hay ascensor?
I ah-sen-SOR?

264. Room service, please.
Servicio de cuarto, por favor.
sayr-VEE-syoh day KWAHR-toh, por fah-VOR.

265. Please send [a porter] to my room.
Haga el favor de mandar [un mozo] a mi cuarto.
AH-gah el fah-VOR day mahn-DAHR [oon MO-so] ah mee KWAHR-toh.

266. —— **a chambermaid.**
una camarera.
OO-nah kah-mah-RAY-rah.

267. —— **a bellhop.**
un botones.
oon bo-TOH-ness.

268. Please call me at nine A.M.
Haga el favor de llamarme a las nueve de la mañana.
AH-gah el fah-VOR day yah-MAHR-may ah lahss NWAY-vay day lah mah-NYAH-nah.

269. I want breakfast in my room.
Quiero el desayuno en mi cuarto.
KYAY-ro el dess-ah-YOO-no en mee KWAHR-toh.

22

270. Who is it?
¿Quién es?
kyen ess?

271. Come back later.
Vuelva más tarde.
VWAYL-vah mahss TAHR-day.

272. Bring me [a blanket].
Tráigame [una frazada].
TRY-gah-may [OO-nah frah-SAH-dah].

273. —— a pillow.
una almohada.
OO-nah ahl-mo-AH-dah.

274. —— a pillowcase.
una funda.
OO-nah FOON-dah.

275. —— some hangers.
ganchos.
GAHN-chohss.

276. —— some soap.
jabón.
hah-BOHN.

277. —— some towels.
toallas.
toh-AH-yahss.

278. —— a bath mat.
un tapete de baño.
oon tah-PAY-tay day BAH-nyoh.

279. —— some toilet paper.
papel higiénico.
pah-PEL ee-HYAY-nee-ko.

280. I should like to speak to the manager.
Quisiera hablar con el gerente.
kee-SYAY-rah ah-BLAHR kohn el hay-REN-tay.

281. My room key, please.
Mi llave, por favor.
mee YAH-vay, por fah-VOR.

282. Have I any letters or messages?
¿Hay cartas o mensajes para mí?
I KAHR-tahss o men-SAH-hess PAH-rah mee?

283. What is my room number?
¿Cuál es el número de mi cuarto?
kwahl ess el NOO-may-ro day mee KWAHR-toh?

284. I am leaving at ten o'clock.
Salgo a las diez.
SAHL-go ah lahss dyayss.

285. Please make out my bill as soon as possible.
Favor de preparar mi cuenta lo más pronto posible.
fah-VOR day pray-pah-RAHR mee KWEN-tah lo mahss PROHN-toh po-SEE-blay.

286. Is everything included?
¿Está todo incluído?
ess-TAH TOH-doh een-kloo-EE-doh?

287. Please forward my mail to American Express in Valparaíso.
Favor de reexpedirme las cartas al American Express en Valparaíso.
fah-VOR day rray-ex-pay-DEER-may lahss KAHR- tahss ahl American Express en vahl-pah-rah-EE-so.

AT THE CAFÉ

288. Bartender, I'd like to have [a drink].
Cantinero, quisiera [una bebida].
kahn-tee-NAY-ro, kee-SYAY-rah [OO-nah bay-BEE- dah].

289. —— a cocktail.
un cocktail.
oon "cocktail."

290. —— a bottle of mineral water.
una botella de agua mineral.
OO-nah bo-TAY-yah day AH-gwah mee-nay-RAHL.

291. —— a glass of sherry.
un vaso de jerez.
oon VAH-so day hay-RAYSS.

292. —— some light (dark) beer.
cerveza clara (oscura).
sayr-VAY-sah KLAH-rah (ohss-KOO-rah).

24

293. —— some red (white) wine.
vino tinto (blanco).
VEE-no TEEN-toh (BLAHN-ko).

294. Let's have another.
Tomemos otro más.
toh-MAY-mohss O-tro mahss.

295. To your health!
¡Salud!
sah-LOOD!

AT THE RESTAURANT

296. Can you recommend a native restaurant [for dinner]?
¿Puede recomendar un restaurante típico [para la comida]?
PWAY-day rray-koh-men-DAHR oon res-tow-RAHN-tay TEE-pee-ko [PAH-rah lah ko-MEE-dah]?

297. —— for breakfast.
para el desayuno.
PAH-rah el dess-ah-YOO-no.

298. —— for lunch.
para el almuerzo.
PAH-rah el ahl-MWAYR-so.

299. —— for a sandwich.
para un sandwich.
PAH-rah oon "sandwich."

300. At what time is supper served?
¿A qué hora se sirve la cena?
ah kay OH-rah say SEER-vay lah SAY-nah?

301. The waitress.
La camarera.
lah kah-mah-RAY-rah.

302. The waiter.
El camarero.
el kah-mah-RAY-ro.

303. The headwaiter.
El jefe de camareros.
el HAY-fay day kah-mah-RAY-rohss.

304. Give me a table for two near the window.
Déme una mesa para dos cerca de la ventana.
DAY-may OO-nah MAY-sah PAH-rah dohss SAYR-kah day lah ven-TAH-nah.

305. We want to dine [à la carte] table d'hôte.
Deseamos comer [a la carta] comida corrida.
day-say-AH-mohss ko-MAYR [ah lah KAHR-tah] ko-MEE-dah ko-RREE-dah.

306. Bring me [the menu].
Tráigame [la carta].
TRY-gah-may [lah KAHR-tah].

307. —— the wine list.
la carta de vinos.
lah KAHR-tah day VEE-nohss.

308. —— a napkin.
una servilleta.
OO-nah sayr-vee-YAY-tah.

309. —— a fork.
un tenedor.
oon tay-nay-DOHR.

310. —— a knife.
un cuchillo.
oon koo-CHEE-yoh.

311. —— a plate.
un plato.
oon PLAH-toh.

312. —— a teaspoon.
una cucharita.
OO-nah koo-chah-REE-tah.

313. —— a large spoon.
una cuchara.
OO-nah koo-CHAH-rah.

314. I want [simple] food.
Quiero comida [sencilla].
KYAY-ro ko-MEE-dah sen-SEE-yah.

315. —— not too fat.
no muy grasosa.
no mwee grah-SO-sah.

316. —— not too sweet.
no muy dulce.
no mwee DOOL-say.

317. —— not too spicy.
no muy condimentada.
no mwee kohn-dee-men-TAH-dah.

318. —— cooked.
cocida.
ko-SEE-dah.

319. —— fried.
frita.
FREE-tah.

320. —— boiled.
hervida.
ayr-VEE-dah.

321. I like the meat [rare].
Me gusta la carne [cruda].
may GOOSS-tah lah KAHR-nay [KROO-dah].

322. —— medium.
mediana.
may-DYAH-nah.

323. —— well done.
bien cocida.
byen ko-SEE-dah.

324. A little more.
Un poco más.
oon PO-ko mahss.

325. Enough.
Suficiente.
soo-fee-SYEN-tay.

326. This is cold.
Esto está frío.
ESS-toh ess-TAH FREE-o.

327. I did not order this.
No he pedido esto.
no ay pay-DEE-doh ESS-toh.

328. Take it away, please.
Lléveselo, por favor.
YAY-vay-say-lo, por fah-VOR.

329. May I change this for a salad?
¿Se puede cambiar esto por una ensalada?
say PWAY-day kahm-BYAHR ESS-toh por OO-nah en-sah-LAH-dah?

330. The check, please.
La cuenta, por favor.
lah KWEN-tah, por fah-VOR.

331. Are the tip and service charge included?
¿Están incluídos la propina y el servicio?
ess-TAHN een-kloo-EE-dohss lah pro-PEE-nah ee el sayr-VEE-syoh?

332. There is a mistake in the bill.
Hay un error en la cuenta.
I oon ay-RROR en lah KWEN-tah.

333. What are these charges for?
¿Qué son estos extras?
kay sohn ESS-tohss EKS-trahss?

334. Keep the change.
Quédese con el cambio.
KAY day-say kohn el KAHM-byoh.

335. The food and service are excellent.
La comida y el servicio son excelentes.
lah ko-MEE-dah ee el sayr-VEE-syoh sohn ek-say-LEN-tays.

336. Hearty appetite!
¡Buen apetito!
bwayn ah-pay-TEE-toh!

FOOD LIST

337. Drinking water.
Agua para beber.
AH-gwah PAH-rah bay-BAYR.

338. —— with ice.
con hielo.
kohn YAY-lo.

339. —— without ice.
sin hielo.
seen YAY-lo.

340. The bread.
El pan.
el pahn.

341. The butter.
La mantequilla.
lah mahn-tay-KEE-yah.

342. The sugar.
El azúcar.
el ah-SOO-kahr.

343. The salt.
La sal.
lah sahl.

344. The pepper.
La pimienta.
lah pee-MYEN-tah.

345. The oil.
El aceite.
el ah-SAY-tay.

346. The vinegar.
El vinagre.
el vee-NAH-gray.

347. The garlic.
El ajo.
el AH-ho.

348. The catsup.
La salsa de tomate.
lah SAHL-sah day toh-MAH-tay.

349. The mustard.
La mostaza.
lah mohss-TAH-sah.

350. The sauce.
La salsa.
lah SAHL-sah.

BREAKFAST FOODS

351. I would like [fruit juice].
Me gustaría [jugo de fruta].
may goos-tah-REE-ah [HOO-go day FROO-tah].

352. —— orange juice.
jugo de naranja.
HOO-go day nah-RAHN-hah.

353. —— tomato juice.
jugo de tomate.
HOO-go day toh-MAH-tay.

354. —— stewed prunes.
ciruelas pasas.
see-RWAY-lahs PAH-sas.

355. —— cooked cereal.
cereal cocido.
say-ree-AHL ko-SEE-doh.

356. —— toast and jam.
tostada con conserva.
tohss-TAH-dah kohn kohn-SAYR-vah.

357. —— rolls.
panecillos.
pah-nay-SEE-yohss.

358. —— an omelet.
una tortilla.
OO-nah tohr-TEE-yah.

359. —— soft-boiled eggs.
huevos tibios.
WAY-vohss TEE-byohss.

360. —— four-minute eggs.
huevos pasados por agua— cuatro minutos.
WAY-vohss pah-SAH-dohss por AH-gwah KWAH-tro mee-NOO-tohss.

361. —— hard-boiled eggs.
huevos duros.
WAY-vohss DOO-rohss.

362. —— fried eggs.
huevos fritos.
WAY-vohss FREE-tohss.

363. —— scrambled eggs.
huevos revueltos.
WAY-vohss rray-VWEL-tohss.

364. —— eggs with bacon.
huevos con tocino.
WAY-vohss kohn toh-SEE-no.

365. —— eggs with ham.
huevos con jamón.
WAY-vohss kohn hah-MOHN.

SOUPS AND ENTRÉES

366. I would like [chicken soup].
Quisiera [sopa de pollo].
kee-see-AY-rah [SO-pah day PO-yo].

367. —— vegetable soup.
sopa de legumbres.
SO-pah day lay-GOOM-brayss.

368. —— anchovies.
anchoas.
ahn-CHO-ahss.

369. —— beef.
carne de vaca.
KAHR-nay day VAH-kah.

370. —— roast beef.
rosbif.
rrohss-BEEF.

371. —— broiled chicken.
pollo a la parrilla.
PO-yo ah lah pah-RREE-yah.

372. —— fried chicken.
pollo frito.
PO-yo FREE-toh.

373. —— duck.
pato.
PAH-toh.

374. —— fish.
pescado.
pess-KAH-doh.

375. —— goose.
ganso.
GAHN-so.

376. —— lamb.
cordero.
kor-DAY-ro.

377. —— liver.
hígado.
EE-gah-doh.

378. —— lobster.
langosta.
lahn-GOHSS-tah.

379. —— oysters.
ostras.
OSS-trahss.

380. —— pork.
puerco.
PWAYR-ko.

381. —— sardines.
sardinas.
sahr-DEE-nahss.

382. —— **sausage.**
salchicha.
sahl-CHEE-chah.

383. —— **shrimp.**
camarones.
kah-mah-RO-ness.

384. —— **steak.**
bisté.
beess-TAY.

385. —— **veal.**
ternera.
tayr-NAY-rah.

VEGETABLES AND SALAD

386. I want some [asparagus].
Quiero [espárragos].
KYAY-ro [ess-PAH-rrah-gohss].

387. —— **beans.**
frijoles.
free-HO-less.

388. —— **cabbage.**
col.
kohl.

389. —— **carrots.**
zanahorias.
sah-nah-OHR-yahss.

390. —— **cauliflower.**
coliflor.
ko-lee-FLOHR.

391. —— **celery and olives.**
apio y aceitunas.
AH-pyoh ee ah-say-TOO-nahss.

392. —— **cucumber.**
pepino.
pay-PEE-noh.

393. —— **lettuce.**
lechuga.
lay-CHOO-gah.

394. —— **mushrooms.**
hongos.
OHN-gohss.

395. —— **onions.**
cebollas.
say-BO-yahss.

396. —— **peas.**
guisantes.
ghee-SAHN-tess.

397. —— **peppers.**
pimientos.
pee-MYEN-tohss.

398. —— **pimentos.**
pimentón.
pee-men-TOHN.

399. —— **boiled potatoes.**
patatas hervidas.
pah-TAH-tahss ayr-VEE-dahss.

400. —— **mashed potatoes.**
puré de papas.
poo-RAY day PAH-pahss.

401. —— **baked potatoes.**
patatas al horno.
pah-TAH-tahss ahl OR-no.

402. —— **fried potatoes.**
patatas fritas.
pah-TAH-tahss FREE-tahss.

403. —— **rice.**
arroz.
ah-RROHSS.

404. —— **spinach.**
espinacas.
ess-pee-NAH-kahss.

405. —— **tomatoes.**
tomates.
toh-MAH-tays.

FRUITS

406. **Do you have [an apple]?**
¿Tiene [una manzana]?
TYAY-nay [OO-nah mahn-SAH-nah]?

407. —— **cherries.**
cerezas.
say-RAY-sahss.

408. —— **a grapefruit.**
una toronja.
OO-nah toh-ROHN-hah.

409. —— **grapes.**
uvas.
OO-vahss.

410. —— **lemon.**
limón.
lee-MOHN.

411. —— **melon.**
melón.
may-LOHN.

412. —— **an orange.**
una naranja.
OO-nah nah-RAHN-hah.

413. —— **a peach.**
un melocotón.
oon may-lo-ko-TOHN.

414. —— **raspberries.**
frambuesas.
frahm-BWAY-sahss.

415. —— **strawberries.**
fresas.
FRAY-sahss.

BEVERAGES

416. A cup of black coffee.
Una taza de café solo.
OO-nah TAH-sah day kah-FAY SO-lo.

417. Coffee with cream.
Café con crema.
kah-FAY kohn KRAY-mah.

418. A glass of milk.
Un vaso de leche.
oon VAH-so day LAY-chay.

419. Tea.
Té.
tay.

420. Lemonade.
Limonada.
lee-mo-NAH-dah.

DESSERTS

421. We would like [some cake].
Quisiéramos [torta].
kee-SYAY-rah-mohss [TOHR-tah].

422. —— a piece of pie.
pastel.
pahs-TEL.

423. —— some cheese.
queso.
KAY-so.

424. —— some cookies.
galletas.
gah-YAY-tahss.

425. —— some custard.
flan.
flahn.

426. —— some chocolate ice cream.
helado de chocolate.
ay-LAH-doh day cho-ko-LAH-tay.

427. —— some vanilla ice cream.
helado de vainilla.
ay-LAH-doh day vie-NEE-yah.

AT THE RESTAURANT

428. ¿Van a tomar algo antes de comer?
Would you like to have something before your dinner?

429. Sí. Un vermouth cassis, un jerez y una botella de vino blanco.
Yes. One vermouth cassis, one glass of sherry, and a bottle of white wine.

430. ¿Quieren pedir la comida ahora mismo?
Do you want to order right now?

431. ¿Qué nos recomienda usted? ¿Cuál es la especialidad de la casa?
What do you recommend? What is the specialty of the house?

432. El bisté está muy bueno hoy. El filete de sol también está muy sabroso.
The beef tenderloin is especially good today. The filet of sole is also very tasty.

433. Un bisté y una langosta.
One beef tenderloin and one lobster.

434. Háganme el favor de elegir dos legumbres.
Please choose two vegetables.

435. Patatas al horno y guisantes con el bisté; cebollas al gratin y espárragos con salsa de mantequilla con la langosta.
Baked potatoes and peas with the beef; onions au gratin and asparagus with butter sauce with the lobster.

436. ¿Y para comenzar?
And to begin with?

437. Arenque en escabeche y un coctel de fruta. Sopa de guisantes y sopa de pollo.
Marinated herring and one fruit cup. Pea soup and chicken soup.

438. ¿Ensalada?
Salad?

439. Sí, una ensalada de lechuga con tomates, aceite y vinagre. No le ponga ajo.
Yes, a lettuce and tomato salad, oil and vinegar. No garlic.

440. ¿Desean tomar café con la comida?
Would you like coffee with your dinner?

441. No. El café lo tomaremos más tarde, con el postre.
No. We'll have coffee later, with the dessert.

442. Muchas gracias.
Thanks.

443. Para postre tenemos: helado de chocolate, vainilla y fresa; pasteles surtidos; queso Camembert y suizo; tartaletas de frambuesa.
For dessert we have: chocolate, vanilla, and strawberry ice cream; assorted pastries; Camembert and Swiss cheese; raspberry tarts.

444. Un helado de chocolate. Una tartaleta de frambuesa. Un café solo. Té con leche. Y camarero, hágame el favor de traerme otra cuchara. Esta no está limpia.
One chocolate ice cream. One raspberry tart. A cup of black coffee. Tea with milk. And waiter, please bring me another spoon. This one isn't clean.

445. Lo siento.
I'm so sorry.

446. La cuenta, por favor. No tenemos mucho tiempo porque vamos al teatro.
The check, please. We don't have much time because we are going to the theatre.

447. Muy bien, señor.
Very well, sir.

CHURCH

448. Is there an English-speaking [priest]?
¿Hay algún [cura] que hable inglés?
I ahl-GOON [KOO-rah] kay AH-blay een-GLAYSS?

449. A rabbi.
Un rabino.
oon rah-BEE-no.

450. A minister.
Un ministro.
oon mee-NEESS-tro.

451. A [Catholic] Protestant church.
Una iglesia [católica] protestante.
OO-nah ee-GLAY-syah [kah-TOH-lee-kah] pro-tess-TAHN-tay.

452. A synagogue.
Una sinagoga.
OO-nah see-nah-GO-gah.

453. When is [the service] the mass?
¿A qué hora es [el servicio] la misa?
ah kay O-rah ess [el sayr-VEE-syoh] lah MEE-sah?

SIGHTSEEING

454. I want a licensed guide who speaks English.
Deseo un guía autorizado que hable inglés.
day-SAY-o oon GHEE-ah ow-toh-ree-SAH-doh kay AH-blay een-GLAYSS.

455. What is the charge [per hour] per day?
¿Cuánto cobra usted [por hora] por día?
KWAHN-toh KO-brah oos-TED [por O-rah] por DEE-ah?

456. I am interested in [architecture].
Me interesa [la arquitectura].
may een-tay-RAY-sah [lah ahr-kee-tek-TOO-rah].

457. —— painting.
la pintura.
lah peen-TOO-rah.

458. —— sculpture.
la escultura.
lah ess-kool-TOO-rah.

36

459. Show us [the castle].
Muéstrenos [el castillo].
MWESS-tray-nohss [el kahss-TEE-yoh].

460. —— the cathedral.
la catedral.
lah kah-tay-DRAHL.

461. —— the museums.
los museos.
lohss moo-SAY-ohss.

462. When does it [open] close?
¿Cuándo se [abre] cierra?
KWAHN-doh say [AH-bray] SYAY-rah?

463. Where is [the entrance]?
¿Dónde está [la entrada]?
DOHN-day ess-TAH [lah en-TRAH-dah]?

464. —— the exit.
la salida.
lah sah-LEE-dah.

AMUSEMENTS

465. I should like to go [to a concert].
Quisiera ir [a un concierto].
kee-SYAY-rah eer [ah oon kohn-SYAYR-toh].

466. —— to a matinée.
a una matinée.
ah OO-nah mah-tee-NAY.

467. —— to the movies.
al cine.
ahl SEE-nay.

468. —— to a night club.
a un cabaret.
ah oon kah-bah-RAY.

469. —— to the opera.
a la ópera.
ah lah O-pay-rah.

470. —— to the theater.
al teatro.
ahl tay-AH-tro.

471. —— to the box office.
a la taquilla.
ah lah tah-KEE-yah.

472. What is playing tonight?
¿Qué dan esta noche?
kay dahn ESS-tah NO-chay?

473. When does [the evening performance] the floor show start?
¿A qué hora comienza [la función de la noche] la revista?
ah kay O-rah ko-MYEN-sah [lah foon-SYOHN day lah NO-chay] lah rray-VEESS-tah?

474. Have you [any seats] for tonight?
¿Hay [localidades] para esta noche?
I [loh-kah-lee-DAH-dayss] PAH-rah ESS-tah NO-chay?

475. —— an orchestra seat.
una luneta.
OO-nah loo-NAY-tah.

476. —— a box.
un palco.
oon PAHL-ko.

477. Can I see well from there?
¿Puedo ver bien desde allí?
PWAY-doh vayr byen DEZ-day ah-YEE?

478. Where can we go to dance?
¿Adónde podemos ir a bailar?
ah-DOHN-day po-DAY-mohss eer ah bie-LAHR?

479. May I have this dance?
¿Me permite esta pieza?
may payr-MEE-tay ESS-tah PYAY-sah?

SPORTS

480. Let's go [to the beach].
Vamos [a la playa].
VAH-mohss [ah la PLAH-yah].

481. —— to the bullfights.
a los toros.
ah lohss TOH-rohss.

482. —— to the horse races.
a las carreras.
ah lahss kah-RRAY-rahss.

483. —— to the jai alai.
al jai-alai.
ahl hie-ah-LIE.

484. —— to the swimming pool.
a la piscina.
ah lah pee-SEE-nah.

485. I'd like to play [golf] tennis.
Me gustaría jugar [golf] tennis.
may gooss-tah-REE-ah hoo-GAHR [golf] TAY-neess.

486. Can we go [fishing]?
¿Podemos ir a [pescar]?
po-DAY-mohss eer ah [pess-KAHR]?

487. —— horseback riding.
montar a caballo.
mohn-TAHR ah kah-BAH-yoh.

488. —— skating.
patinar.
pah-tee-NAHR.

489. —— swimming.
nadar.
nah-DAHR.

BANK AND MONEY

490. Where is the nearest bank?
¿Dónde está el banco más cercano?
DOHN-day ess-TAH el BAHN-ko mahss sayr-KAH-no?

491. At which window can I cash this?
¿En qué ventanilla puedo cobrar esto?
en kay ven-tah-NEE-yah PWAY-doh ko-BRAHR ESS-toh?

492. Will you cash [a personal check]?
¿Quiere usted cobrarme [un cheque personal]?
KYAY-ray ooss-TED ko-BRAHR-may [oon CHAY- kay payr-so-NAHL]?

493. —— a traveler's check.
un cheque de viajero.
oon CHAY-kay day vyah-HAY-ro.

494. What is the exchange rate on the dollar?
¿A cómo está el cambio del dólar?
ah KO-mo ess-TAH el KAHM-byoh del DOH-lahr?

495. Can you change this for me?
¿Puede usted cambiarme esto?
PWAY-day ooss-TED kahm-BYAHR-may ESS-toh?

496. I want [the equivalent of fifty dollars].
Quisiera [el equivalente de cincuenta dólares].
kee-SYAY-rah [el ay-kee-vah-LEN-tay day seen-KWEN-tah DOH-lah-ress].

497. —— small change.
cambio.
KAHM-byoh.

SHOPPING

498. I want to go shopping.
Deseo ir de compras.
day-SAY-o eer day KOHM-prahss.

499. I like this one.
Me gusta éste.
may GOOSS-tah ESS-tay.

500. How much is it?
¿Cuánto es?
KWAHN-toh ess?

501. I prefer something [better].
Prefiero algo [mejor].
pray-FYAY-ro AHL-go [may-HOR].

502. —— cheaper.
más barato.
mahss bah-RAH-toh.

503. —— larger.
más grande.
mahss GRAHN-day.

504. —— smaller.
más pequeño.
mahss pay-KAY-nyoh.

505. May I try this on?
¿Me permite probarme esto?
may payr-MEE-tay pro-BAHR-may ESS-toh?

506. Can I order size 38?
¿Puedo mandar hacer de talla treinta y ocho?
PWAY-doh mahn-DAHR ah-SAYR day TAH-yah TRAYN-tah ee O-cho?

507. Please take [the measurements].
Haga el favor de tomarme [las medidas].
AH-gah el fah-VOR day toh-MAHR-may [lahss may-DEE-dahss].

508. —— **the length.**
el largo.
el LAHR-go.

509. —— **the width.**
el ancho.
el AHN-cho.

510. How long will it take?
¿Cuánto tardará?
KWAHN-toh tahr-dah-RAH?

511. Can you ship it to New York City?
¿Puede mandarlo a Nueva York?
PWAY-day mahn-DAHR-lo ah NWAY-vah york?

512. Do I pay [the salesgirl]?
¿Le pago [a la dependienta]?
lay PAH-go [ah lah day-pen-DYEN-tah]?

513. —— **the salesman.**
al dependiente.
ahl day-pen-DYEN-tay.

514. —— **the cashier.**
al cajero.
ahl kah-HAY-ro.

515. Please bill me.
Favor de cargarlo a mi cuenta.
fah-VOR day kahr-GAHR-lo ah mee KWEN-tah.

SHOPPING LIST

516. I want to buy [a bathing cap].
Quiero comprar [un gorro de baño].
KYAY-ro kohm-PRAHR [oon GO-rro day BAH-nyoh].

517. —— **a bathing suit.**
un traje de baño.
oon TRAH-hay day BAH-nyoh.

518. —— **a blouse.**
una blusa.
OO-nah BLOO-sah.

519. —— **a brassiere.**
un sostén.
oon sohss-TEN.

520. —— **a topcoat.**
un abrigo.
oon ah-BREE-go.

521. —— **a dress.**
un vestido.
oon vess-TEE-doh.

522. —— **a pair of gloves.**
un par de guantes.
oon pahr day GWAHN-tess.

523. —— **a handbag.**
una bolsa.
OO-nah BOHL-sah.

524. —— **one dozen handkerchiefs.**
una docena de pañuelos.
OO-nah doh-SAY-nah day pah-NWAY-lohss.

525. —— **a hat.**
un sombrero.
oon sohm-BRAY-ro.

526. —— **a jacket.**
una chaqueta.
OO-nah chah-KAY-tah.

527. —— **a nightgown.**
un camisón.
oon kah-mee-SOHN.

528. —— **a raincoat.**
un impermeable.
oon eem-payr-may-AH-blay.

529. —— **a pair of shoes.**
un par de zapatos.
oon pahr day sah-PAH-tohss.

530. —— **shoelaces.**
cintas de zapatos.
SEEN-tahss day sah-PAH-tohss.

531. —— **a skirt.**
una falda.
OO-nah FAHL-dah.

532. —— **a pair of slippers.**
un par de zapatillas.
oon pahr day sah-pah-TEE-yahss.

533. —— **a pair of socks.**
un par de calcetines.
oon pahr day kahl-say-TEE-ness.

534. —— **a pair of nylon stockings.**
un par de medias nylon.
oon pahr day MAY-dyahss nie-LOHN.

535. —— **a suit.**
un traje.
oon TRAH-hay.

536. —— **a sweater.**
un suéter.
oon SWAY-tayr.

537. —— **neckties.**
corbatas.
kor-BAH-tahss.

538. —— **a pair of trousers.**
un par de pantalones.
oon pahr day pahn-tah-LO-ness.

539. —— **underwear.**
ropa interior.
RRO-pah een-teh-RYOR.

540. Do you have [ashtrays]?
¿Tiene [ceniceros]?
TYAY-nay [say-nee-SAY-rohss]?

541. —— **artist's supplies.**
material para artistas.
mah-tay-RYAHL PAH-rah ahr-TEES-tahs.

542. —— **a box of candy.**
una caja de dulces.
OO-nah KAH-hah day DOOL-sayss.

543. —— **china.**
loza.
LOH-sah.

544. —— **a silver compact.**
una polvera de plata.
OO-nah pohl-VAY-rah day PLAH-tah.

545. —— **gold cuff links.**
gemelos de oro.
hay-MAY-lohss day O-ro.

546. —— **dolls.**
muñecas.
moo-NYAY-kahss.

547. —— **earrings.**
aretes.
ah-RAY-tayss.

548. —— **musical instruments.**
instrumentos musicales.
een-stroo MEN-tohss moo-see-KAH-layss.

549. —— perfume.
perfume.
payr-FOO-may.

550. —— pictures.
cuadros.
KWAH-drohss.

551. —— records.
discos.
DEES-kohss.

552. —— silverware.
platería.
plah-tay-REE-ah.

553. —— souvenirs.
recuerdos.
ray-KWEHR-dohss.

554. —— toys.
juguetes.
hoo-GAY-tayss.

555. —— an umbrella.
un paraguas.
oon pah-RAH-gwahss.

556. —— a watch.
un reloj.
oon rray-LOH.

COLORS

557. I want [a lighter shade].
Quiero [un tono más claro].
KYAY-ro [oon TOH-no mahss KLAH-ro].

558. —— a darker shade.
un tono más oscuro.
oon TOH-no mahss ohss-KOO-ro.

559. —— black.
negro.
NAY-gro.

560. —— blue.
azul.
ah-SOOL.

561. —— brown.
café.
kah-FAY.

562. —— gray.
gris.
greess.

563. —— green.
verde.
VAYR-day.

564. —— orange.
anaranjado.
ah-nah-rahn-HAH-doh.

565. —— pink.
rosado.
rro-SAH-doh.

566. —— purple.
morado.
mo-RAH-doh.

567. —— red.
rojo.
RRO-ho.

568. —— white.
blanco.
BLAHN-ko.

569. —— **yellow.**
amarillo.
ah-mah-REE-yoh.

STORES

570. Where is [a bakery]?
¿Dónde hay [una panadería]?
DOHN-day I [OO-nah pah-nah-day-REE-ah]?

571. —— **a candy store.**
una dulcería.
OO-nah dool-say-REE-ah.

572. —— **a cigar store.**
una cigarrería.
OO-nah see-gah-rray-REE-ah.

573. —— **a clothing store.**
una tienda de ropa.
OO-nah TYEN-dah day RRO-pah.

574. —— **a department store.**
un almacén.
oon ahl-mah-SEN.

575. —— **a drugstore.**
una farmacia.
OO-nah fahr-MAH-syah.

576. —— **a grocery.**
una tienda de comestibles.
OO-nah TYEN-dah day ko-mess-TEE-blayss.

577. —— **a hardware store.**
una ferretería.
OO-nah fay-rray-tay-REE-ah.

578. —— **a hat shop.**
una sombrerería.
OO-nah sohm-bray-ray-REE-ah.

579. —— **a jewelry store.**
una joyería.
OO-nah ho-yay-REE-ah.

580. —— **a market.**
un mercado.
oon mayr-KAH-doh.

581. —— **a meat market.**
una carnicería.
OO-nah kahr-nee-say-REE-ah.

582. —— **a pastry shop.**
una panadería.
OO-nah pah-nah-day-REE-ah.

583. —— **a shoemaker.**
un zapatero.
oon sah-pah-TAY-ro.

584. —— **a shoe store.**
una zapatería.
OO-nah sah-pah-tay-REE-ah.

585. —— **a tailor shop.**
una sastrería.
OO-nah sahss-tray-REE-ah.

586. —— **a watchmaker.**
un relojero.
oon rray-lo-HAY-ro.

BOOKSTORE AND STATIONER'S

587. Where is there [a bookstore]?
¿Dónde hay [una librería]?
DOHN-day I [OO-nah lee-bray-REE-ah]?

588. —— **a news dealer.**
un expendio de periódicos.
oon ess-PAYN-dyoh day pay-RYOH-dee-kohss.

589. —— **a stationer's.**
una papelería.
OO-nah pah-pay-lay-REE-ah.

590. I want to buy [a book].
Quiero comprar [un libro].
KYAY-ro kohm-PRAHR [oon LEE-bro].

591. —— **a guidebook.**
una guía.
OO-nah GHEE-ah.

592. —— **a dictionary.**
un diccionario.
oon deek-syoh-NAH-ryoh.

593. —— **a magazine.**
una revista.
OO-nah rray-VEESS-tah.

594. —— **a map of Mexico.**
un mapa de México.
oon MAH-pah day MAY-hee-ko.

595. —— **a newspaper.**
un periódico.
oon pay-RYOH-dee-koh.

596. I would like [some envelopes].
Quisiera [sobres].
kee-see-AY-rah [SO-bress].

597. —— **some ink.**
tinta.
TEEN-tah.

598. —— **some writing paper.**
papel para cartas.
pah-PEL PAH-rah KAHR-tahss.

599. —— **a fountain pen.**
una plumafuente.
OO-nah PLOO-mah-FWEN-tay.

600. —— **a pencil.**
un lápiz.
oon LAH-peess.

601. —— **some postcards.**
tarjetas postales.
tahr-HAY-tahss pohss-TAH-less.

602. —— **some wrapping paper.**
papel para envolver.
pah-PEL PAH-rah en-vohl-VAYR.

603. —— **some string.**
cuerda.
KWAYR-dah.

CIGAR STORE

604. Where is the nearest cigar store?
¿Dónde está la tabaquería más cercana?
DOHN-day ess-TAH lah tah-bah-kay-REE-ah mahss sayr-KAH-nah?

605. I want [some cigars].
Deseo [unos puros].
day-SAY-o [OO-nohss POO-rohss].

606. —— a pack of American cigarettes.
un paquete de cigarrillos americanos.
oon pah-KAY-tay day see-gah-RREE-yohss ah-may-ree-KAH-nohss.

607. —— a leather cigarette case.
una cigarrera de cuero.
OO-nah see-gah-RRAY-rah day KWAY-ro.

608. —— a lighter.
un encendedor.
oon en-sen-day-DOR.

609. —— some pipe tobacco.
tabaco de pipa.
tah-BAH-ko day PEE-pah.

610. Do you have a match?
¿Tiene un fósforo?
TYAY-nay oon FOSS-fo-ro?

CAMERA SHOP

611. I want a roll of movie film for this camera.
Quiero un rollo de película de cine para esta cámara.
*KYAY-ro oon RRO-yo day pay-LEE-koo-lah day SEE-nay PAH-rah
ESS-tah KAH-mah-rah.*

612. What is the charge for developing a roll of color film?
¿Cuánto cuesta revelar un rollo de película de color?
*KWAHN-toh KWESS-tah rray-vay-LAHR oon RRO- yoh day pay-LEE-koo-lah
day ko-LOHR?*

613. When will they be ready?
¿Cuándo estarán listas?
KWAHN-doh ess-tah-RAHN LEESS-tahss?

614. May I take a snapshot of you?
¿Me permite sacarle una foto?
may payr-MEE-tay sah-KAHR-lay OO-nah FO-toh?

DRUGSTORE

615. Where is there a drugstore where they understand English?
¿Dónde hay una farmacia donde entiendan inglés?
DOHN-day I OO-nah fahr-MAH-syah DOHN-day ayn-TYEN-dahn een-GLAYSS?

616. Can you fill this prescription immediately?
¿Puede prepararme esta receta en seguida?
PWAY-day pray-pah-RAHR-may ESS-tah rray-SAY- tah en say-GHEE-dah?

617. Do you have [adhesive tape]?
¿Tiene [esparadrapo]?
TYAY-nay [ess-pah-rah-DRAH-po]?

618. —— alcohol.
alcohol.
ahl-KOHL.

619. —— antiseptic.
antiséptico.
ahn-tee-SEP-tee-ko.

620. —— aspirin.
aspirina.
ahss-pee-REE-nah.

621. —— an ice bag.
un saquito para hielo.
oon sah-KEE-toh PAH-rah YAY-lo.

622. —— a hairbrush.
un cepillo.
oon say-PEE-yoh.

623. —— a toothbrush.
un cepillo de dientes.
oon say-PEE-yoh day DYEN-tess.

624. —— cold cream.
crema para la cara.
KRAY-mah PAH-rah lah KAH-rah.

625. —— a comb.
un peine.
oon PAY-nay.

626. —— corn pads.
parches para callos.
PAHR-chess PAH-rah KAH-yohss.

627. —— cotton.
algodón.
ahl-go-DOHN.

628. —— a deodorant.
un desodorante.
oon dess-o-doh-RAHN-tay.

629. —— cleaning fluid.
quitamanchas.
kee-tah-MAHN-chahss.

630. —— iodine.
yodo.
YO-doh.

631. —— a mild laxative.
un laxante suave.
oon lak-SAHN-tay SWAH-vay.

632. —— lipstick.
lápiz de labios.
LAH-peess day LAH-byohss.

633. —— powder.
polvos.
POHL-vohss.

634. —— rouge.
colorete.
ko-lo-RAY-tay.

635. —— hairpins.
horquillas.
or-KEE-yahss.

636. —— a razor.
una navaja de afeitar.
OO-nah nah-VAH-hah day ah-fay-TAHR.

637. —— razor blades.
hojas de afeitar.
O-hahss day ah-fay-TAHR.

638. —— sanitary napkins.
toallas higiénicas.
toh-AH-yahss ee-HYAY-nee-kahss.

639. —— a sedative.
un sedante.
oon say-DAHN-tay.

640. —— shampoo.
shampoo.
shahm-POO.

641. —— a shaving lotion.
una loción para después de afeitar.
OO-nah lo-SYOHN PAH-rah dess-PWAYSS day ah-fay-TAHR.

642. —— **(brushless) shaving cream.**
crema de afeitar (sin brocha).
KRAY-mah day ah-fay-TAHR (seen BRO- chah).

643. —— **sunglasses.**
lentes oscuros.
LEN-tess ohss-KOO-rohss.

644. —— **suntan oil.**
loción contra quemadura de sol.
lo-SYOHN KOHN-trah kay-mah-DOO-rah day sohl.

645. —— **a thermometer.**
un termómetro.
oon tayr-MO-may-tro.

646. —— **a tube of toothpaste.**
un tubo de pasta para los dientes.
oon TOO-bo day PAHSS-tah PAH-rah lohss DYEN-tess.

LAUNDRY AND DRY CLEANING

647. Where is [the laundry]?
¿Dónde está [la lavandería]?
DOHN-day ess-TAH [lah lah-vahn-day-REE-ah]?

648. —— **the dry cleaner?**
la tintorería?
lah teen-toh-ray-REE-ah?

649. I want these shirts [washed] mended.
Quiero que me [laven] remienden estas camisas.
KYAY-ro kay may [LAH-ven] rray-MYEN-den ESS-tahss kah-MEE-sahss.

650. Without starch.
Sin almidón.
seen ahl-mee-DOHN.

651. I want this suit [cleaned] pressed.
Quiero que me [limpien] planchen este traje.
KYAY-ro kay may [LEEM-pyen] PLAHN-chehn ESS-tay TRAH-hay.

652. The belt is missing.
Falta el cinturón.
FAHL-tah el seen-too-ROHN.

653. Can you sew on this button?
¿Puede coserme este botón?
PWAY-day ko-SAYR-may ESS-tay bo-TOHN?

654. Repair the zipper.
Compóngame el cierre.
kohm-POHN-gah-may el SYAY-rray.

BARBER SHOP AND BEAUTY PARLOR

655. Where is there [a good beauty parlor]?
¿Dónde hay [un buen salón de belleza]?
DOHN-day I [oon bwen sah-LOHN day bay-YAY- sah]?

656. —— a good barber shop.
una buena peluquería.
OO-nah BWEN-ah pay-loo-kay-REE-ah.

657. May I have a haircut, please?
Quiero una cortada de pelo, por favor.
KYAY-ro OO-nah kor-TAH-dah day PAY-lo, por fah-VOR?

658. Not too short.
No demasiado corto.
no day-mah-SYAH-doh KOR-toh.

659. No lotion, please.
No me ponga loción, por favor.
no may POHN-gah loh-SYOHN, por fah-VOR.

660. May I have [a shave]?
¿Me quiere dar [una afeitada]?
may KYAY-ray dahr [OO-nah ah-fay-TAH-dah]?

661. —— a shampoo.
un shampoo.
oon shahm-POO.

662. —— a permanent.
una permanente.
OO-nah payr-mah-NEN-tay.

663. —— **a manicure.**
un manicure.
oon mah-nee-KOO-ray.

664. —— **a facial.**
un masaje facial.
oon mah-SAH-hay fah-SYAHL.

665. —— **a massage.**
un masaje.
oon mah-SAH-hay.

666. —— **a shoeshine.**
una lustrada de zapatos.
OO-nah looss-TRAH-dah day sah-PAH-tohss.

HEALTH AND ILLNESS

667. I wish to see an American doctor.
Deseo ver a un médico norteamericano.
day-SAY-o vayr ah oon MAY-dee-ko nor-tay-ah-may- ree-KAH-no.

668. Is the doctor in?
¿Está el doctor?
ess-TAH el dok-TOHR?

669. I have [a headache].
Tengo [dolor de cabeza].
TEN-go [doh-LOHR day kah-BAY-sah].

670. —— **a cold.**
catarro.
kah-TAH-rro.

671. —— **a cough.**
tos.
tohss.

672. —— **constipation.**
estreñimiento.
ess-tray-nyee-MYEN-toh.

673. —— **diarrhea.**
diarrea.
dyah-RRAY-ah.

674. —— **indigestion.**
indigestión.
een-dee-hess-TYOHN.

675. —— **fever.**
calentura.
kah-len-TOO-rah.

676. —— nausea.
náuseas.
NOW-say-ahss.

677. —— a sore throat.
inflamación de la garganta.
een-flah-mah-SYOHN day lah gahr-GAHN-tah.

678. **There is something in my eye.**
Tengo algo en el ojo.
TEN-go AHL-go en el O-ho.

679. **I have a pain in my chest.**
Tengo un dolor en el pecho.
TEN-go oon doh-LOHR en el PAY-cho.

680. **I do not sleep well.**
No duermo bien.
no DWAYR-mo byen.

681. **Must I stay in bed?**
¿Tengo que guardar cama?
TEN-go kay gwahr-DAHR KAH-mah?

682. **When can I travel?**
¿Cuándo puedo viajar?
KWAHN-doh PWAY-doh vyah-HAHR?

DENTIST

683. **Do you know a good dentist?**
¿Conoce a un buen dentista?
ko-NO-say ah oon bwen den-TEESS-tah?

684. **This tooth hurts.**
Me duele este diente.
may DWAY-lay ESS-tay DYEN-tay.

685. **Can you fix it temporarily?**
¿Puede usted componerlo por ahora?
PWAY-day oos-TED kohm-po-NAYR-lo por ah-O-rah?

686. I have lost a filling.
Perdí una tapadura.
payr-DEE OO-nah tah-pah-DOO-rah.

687. I do not want the tooth extracted.
No deseo que me saque el diente.
no day-SAY-o kay may SAH-kay el DYEN-tay.

TELEPHONING

688. Where can I telephone?
¿Dónde puedo telefonear?
DOHN-day PWAY-doh tay-lay-fo-nay-AHR?

689. Will you telephone for me?
¿Quiere telefonear de mi parte?
KYAY-ray tay-lay-fo-nay-AHR day mee PAHR-tay?

690. I want to make a local call, number 20-36-48.
Quiero hacer una llamada local, el número es el veinte—treinta y seis—cuarenta y ocho.
KYAY-ro ah-SAYR OO-nah yah-MAH-dah lo-KAHL, el NOO-may-ro es el VAYN-tay—TRAYN-tah ee sayss—kwah-REN-tah ee OH-cho.

691. Give me the long-distance operator.
Comuníqueme con la operadora de larga distancia.
ko-moo-NEE-kay-may kohn lah oh-pay-rah-DOH-rah day LAHR-gah deess-TAHN-syah.

692. My number is 20-28-67.
Hablo del veinte—veinte y ocho—sesenta y siete.
AH-bloh del VAYN-tay—VAYN-tay ee OH-cho—say-SEN-tah ee SYAY-tay.

693. May I speak to Pedro?
¿Me permite hablar con Pedro?
may payr-MEE-tay ah-BLAHR kohn PAY-dro?

694. This is Carlos.
Habla Carlos.
AH-blah KAHR-lohss.

695. Please take a message for me.
Hágame el favor de tomar un mensaje.
AH-gah-may el fah-VOHR day toh-MAHR oon men-SAH-hay.

AT THE POST OFFICE

696. Quisiera mandar esta carta a los Estados Unidos. ¿Cuántos sellos lleva?
I'd like to send this letter to the United States. How many stamps does it take?

697. Por correo ordinario, veinte centavos. Por correo aéreo, cincuenta centavos por cada cinco gramos.
By regular mail, 20 centavos. By airmail, 50 centavos for each 5 grams.

698. Déme diez sellos de a veinte centavos y cinco de a cincuenta.
Give me ten 20-centavo stamps and five 50-centavo stamps.

699. Aquí los tiene. Cuatro pesos, cincuenta centavos, por favor.
Here they are. Four pesos and fifty centavos, please.

700. Muchas gracias. ¿Dónde puedo mandar este paquete por correo?
Thank you. Where can I send this package parcel post?

701. Yo puedo atenderlo. ¿Qué contiene?
I can take care of it. What does it contain?

702. Unos libros.
A few books.

703. ¿Son nuevos?
Are they new?

704. No. ¿Los puedo asegurar? ¿Cuánto cuesta el seguro?
No. Can I insure them? How much is the insurance?

705. Diez centavos por cada cincuenta pesos de seguro.
Ten centavos per 50 pesos of insurance.

706. Quisiera asegurarlos por veinte y cinco pesos.
I should like to insure them for 25 pesos.

707. Hágame el favor de llenar esta forma. El importe total es de un peso, siete centavos — ochenta y dos centavos de correo y veinte y cinco centavos por el seguro.
Please fill out this form. The total charge is 1 peso, 7 centavos—82 centavos for postage and 25 centavos for insurance.

708. ¿Me da un recibo?
Will you give me a receipt?

709. Sí, señor. Hágame el favor de firmar aquí. A su derecha hay un buzón.
Yes, sir. Please sign your name here. To your right is a mail chute.

710. Muchas gracias.
Thanks very much.

SENDING A TELEGRAM

711. Quisiera mandar un telegrama a Nueva York. ¿Cuánto cuesta por palabra?
I'd like to send a cablegram to New York City. What is the rate per word?

712. En un telegrama ordinario la tarifa es de diez y ocho centavos por palabra.
Regular cablegram is 18 centavos per word.

713. ¿Hay el mínimo corriente de diez palabras?
Is there the usual ten-word minimum?

714. No, señor, no hay un mínimo.
No, sir, there is no minimum charge.

715. ¿Se puede enviar una carta nocturna?
Can I send a night letter?

716. **Sí. Cuesta la mitad pero se cobra un mínimo de veintidos palabras.**
Yes, at a one-half rate, but there is a 22-word minimum charge.

717. **¿Cuándo llegaría una carta nocturna?**
When would a night letter arrive?

718. **Hasta mañana en la tarde.**
Not until tomorrow afternoon.

719. **¿Cuándo llegaría un cable?**
When would a cablegram arrive?

720. **Dentro de cinco horas.**
Within five hours.

721. **Voy a mandar un cable ordinario. ¿Me permite unas formas?**
I'll send a regular cablegram. May I have some forms?

722. **Aquí las tiene. Tenga la bondad de escribir su nombre completo y su dirección en letras de imprenta. Una vez hecho esto, tendré mucho gusto en atenderle.**
Here they are. Please print your full name and address. When you've done this, I'll be glad to take care of you.

723. **Muchísimas gracias.**
Thanks very much.

TIME AND TIME EXPRESSIONS

724. What time is it?
¿Qué hora es?
kay O-rah ess?

725. It is early.
Es temprano.
ess tem-PRAH-no.

726. It is (too) late.
Ya es (muy) tarde.
yah ess (mwee) TAHR-day.

727. It is two o'clock [A.M.].
Son las dos [de la mañana].
sohn lahss dohss [day lah mah-NYAH-nah].

728. —— P.M.
de la tarde.
day lah TAHR-day.

729. It is half-past three.
Son las tres y media.
sohn lahss trayss ee MAY-dyah.

730. It is quarter-past four.
Son las cuatro y cuarto.
sohn lahss KWAH-tro ee KWAHR-toh.

731. It is a quarter to five.
Son las cinco menos cuarto.
sohn lahss SEEN-ko MAY-nohss KWAHR-toh.

732. At ten minutes to six.
A las seis menos diez.
ah lahss sayss MAY-nohss dyess.

733. At twenty minutes past six.
A las seis y veinte.
ah lahss sayss ee VAYN-tay.

734. In the morning.
Por la mañana.
por lah mah-NYAH-nah.

735. In the afternoon.
Por la tarde.
por lah TAHR-day.

736. In the evening.
Por la noche.
por lah NO-chay.

737. Day.
El día.
el DEE-ah.

738. Night.
La noche.
lah NO-chay.

739. Last night.
Anoche.
ah-NO-chay.

740. Yesterday.
Ayer.
ah-YAYR.

741. Today.
Hoy.
oy.

742. Tonight.
Esta noche.
ESS-tah NO-chay.

743. Tomorrow.
Mañana.
mah-NYAH-nah.

744. Next week.
La semana próxima.
luh suy-MAH-nah PROHK-see-mah

DAYS OF THE WEEK

745. Monday.
Lunes.
LOO-ness.

746. Tuesday.
Martes.
MAHR-tess.

747. Wednesday.
Miércoles.
mee-AYR-ko-less.

748. Thursday.
Jueves.
HWAY-vess.

749. Friday.
Viernes.
vee-AYR-ness.

750. Saturday.
Sábado.
SAH-bah-doh.

751. Sunday.
Domingo.
doh-MEEN-go.

MONTHS AND SEASONS

752. January.
Enero.
ay-NAY-ro.

753. February.
Febrero.
fay-BRAY-ro.

754. March.
Marzo.
MAHR-so.

755. April.
Abril.
ah-BREEL.

756. May.
Mayo.
MAH-yoh.

757. June.
Junio.
HOO-nyoh.

758. July.
Julio.
HOO-lyoh.

759. August.
Agosto.
ah-GOHSS-toh.

760. September.
Septiembre.
sep-TYEM-bray.

761. October.
Octubre.
ok-TOO-bray.

762. November.
Noviembre.
no-VYEM-bray.

763. December.
Diciembre.
dee-SYEM-bray.

764. Spring.
La primavera.
lah pree-mah-VAY-rah.

765. Summer.
El verano.
el vay-RAH-no

766. Autumn.
El otoño.
el o-TOH-nyoh.

767. Winter.
El invierno.
el een-vee-AYR-no.

768. Today is Friday, September first.
Hoy es viernes, primero de septiembre.
oy ess vee-AYR-ness, pree-MAY-ro day sep-TYEM-bray.

WEATHER

769. It is warm.
Hace calor.
AH-say kah-LOHR.

770. It is cold.
Hace frío.
AH-say FREE-o.

771. The weather is [good] bad.
Hace [buen] mal tiempo.
AH-say [bwen] mahl TYEM-po.

772. It is raining.
Llueve.
yoo-AY-vay.

NUMBERS

773. One. Uno. *OO-no.*

Two. Dos. *dohss.*

Three. Tres. *trayss.*

Four. Cuatro. *KWAH-tro.*

Five. Cinco. *SEEN-ko.*

Six. Seis. *sayss.*

Seven. Siete. *SYAY-tay.*

Eight. Ocho. *O-cho.*

Nine. Nueve. *NWAY-vay.*

Ten. Diez. *dyess.*

Eleven. Once. *OHN-say.*

Twelve. Doce. *DOH-say.*

Thirteen. Trece. *TRAY-say.*

Fourteen. Catorce. *kah-TOR-say.*

Fifteen. Quince. *KEEN-say.*

Sixteen. Diez y seis. *dyess ee sayss.*

Seventeen. Diez y siete. *dyess ee SYAY-tay.*

Eighteen. Diez y ocho. *dyess ee O-cho.*

Nineteen. Diez y nueve. *dyess ee NWAY-vay.*

Twenty. Veinte. *VAYN-tay*.

Twenty-one. Veintiuno. *vayn-tee-OO-no*.

Twenty-two. Veintidós. *vayn-tee-DOHSS*.

Thirty. Treinta. *TRAYN-tah*.

Thirty-one. Treinta y uno. *TRAYN-tah ee OO-no*.

Forty. Cuarenta. *kwah-REN-tah*.   **Fifty.** Cincuenta. *seen-KWEN-tah*.

Sixty. Sesenta. *say-SEN-tah*.   **Seventy.** Setenta. *say-TEN-tah*.

Seventy-one. Setenta y uno. *say-TEN-tah ee OO-no*.

Eighty. Ochenta. *o-CHEN-tah*.

Eighty-one. Ochenta y uno. *o-CHEN-tah ee OO-no*.

Ninety. Noventa. *no-VEN-tah*.

Ninety-one. Noventa y uno. *no-VEN-tah ee OO-no*.

Ninety-two. Noventa y dos. *no-VEN-tah ee dohss*.

One hundred. Cien. *syen*.

Two hundred. Doscientos. *dohss-SYEN-tohss*.

Five hundred. Quinientos. *kee-NYEN-tohss*.

Seven hundred. Setecientos. *say-tay-SYEN- tohss*.

Nine hundred. Novecientos. *no-vay-SYEN- tohss*.

One thousand. Mil. *meel*.   **Two thousand.** Dos mil. *dohss meel*.

One million. Un millón. *oon mee-LYOHN*.

INDEX

The sentences, words and phrases in this book are numbered consecutively from 1 to 773. All entries in this book refer to these numbers. In addition, each major section heading (CAPITALIZED) is indexed according to page number (**boldface**). Parts of speech are indicated by the following italic abbreviations: *adj.* for adjective, *adv.* for adverb, *n.* for noun and *v.* for verb. Parentheses are used for explanations.

Because of the large volume of material indexed, cross-indexing has generally been avoided. Phrases or groups of words will usually be found under only one of their components, e.g., "bathing suit" appears only under "bathing," even though there is a separate entry for "suit" alone. If you do not find a phrase under one word, try another.

better 501
BEVERAGES **p. 32**
bill (*n.*, = check) 332; *v.* 515
black 559
blanket 272
blouse 518
blue 560
board, go on 172
boarding house 242
BOAT **p. 13**
boiled 320
bon voyage 173
book *n.* 590, 702
bookstore 587
BOOKSTORE AND STATIONER'S **p. 45**
bottle 290
box 542; (seat) 476; — office 471
boy 74
brake 232
brassiere 519
bread 340
breakfast 269
BREAKFAST FOODS **p. 27**
bring 272, 444
broiled 371
broken 101
brother 13
brown 561
bullfight 481
bus 203; — service 183; — stop 200
BUS AND STREETCAR **p. 15**
businessman 41
business trip 43
butter 341
button 653
buy 516

Cabbage 388
cabin 177
cablegram 711, 721
CAFÉ, AT THE **p. 23**
cake 421
call *n.* 690; *v.* 208; — on 30
camera 611
CAMERA SHOP **p. 47**
can *v.* 95, 158
candy 542; — store 571
captain 174
car 216, 231

carefully (= with care) 213
carrot 389
cash *v.* 429, 491
cashier 514
castle 459
cathedral 460
Catholic 451
catsup 348
cauliflower 390
celery 391
cereal 355
chambermaid 266
change *v.* 229, 495; (= exchange) 329; (= transfer) 205
charge *n.* 707; minimum — 714; service — 331; what is the — 612; *v.* 210
cheaper 502
check *n.* (bank) 492; (= bill) 330; traveler's — 493; *v.* (baggage) 122; (= examine) 233
cheese 423
cherry 407
chest 679
chicken 371
child 16
china 543
chocolate 426
choose 434
Christmas 35
CHURCH **p. 35**
cigar 605
cigarette 606; — case 607
CIGAR STORE **p. 46**
cigar store 604
circle 204
citizen 37
city 134
class 164
clean *adj.* 444; *v.* 651
cleaning fluid 629
close *v.* 193, 462
clothing 116; — store 573
cocktail 289
coffee 416
cold *adj.* 326; — cream 624; I am — 47; it is — 770; *n.* 670
COLORS **p. 43**
comb 625
come 28, 184; — back 271; — here 89; — in 90

compact *n.* 544
concert 465
congratulations 32
constipation 672
consulate 106
contain 701
cooked 318, 355
cookie 424
corner 149
corn pads 626
cotton 627
cough *n.* 671
cream 417
cucumber 392
cuff links 545
cup 416
custard 425
CUSTOMS **p. 8**
customs 107

Dance *v.* 478
dark 292
darker 558
daughter 9
day 737
DAYS OF THE WEEK **p. 59**
December 763
deck 178
declare (customs) 113
DENTIST **p. 53**
dentist 683
department store 574
dessert 441
DESSERTS **p. 32**
develop 612
diarrhea 673
dictionary 592
DIFFICULTIES **p. 6**
dine 305
diner (= dining car) 195
dinner 296
direct *adj.* 131
do 100
dock 180
doctor 667, 668
doll 546
dollar 494, 496
downstairs 262
dozen 524
dress 521
drink *n.* 288
drive 212
driver 206
driver's license 217
DRUGSTORE **p. 48**
drugstore 575

pea 396; — soup 437
peach 413
pen, fountain 599
pencil 600
pepper (seasoning) 344; (vegetable) 397
per 187
performance 473
perfume 549
permanent n. 662
person 252
personal 114
picture 550
pie 422
pillow 273
pillowcase 274
pimentos 398
pink 565
pipe 609
plate 311
play v. 485
playing, what is 472
plaza 199
please 25, 59, 722
P.M. (= in the afternoon) 728
policeman 105
police station 104
pork 380
postage 707
postcard 601
POST OFFICE, AT THE p. 55
potato 399–402
powder 633
prefer 501
prescription 616
press v. 651
priest 448
Protestant 451
prune 354
puncture n. 235
purple 566
purse 97
purser 175
put 126

Quarter: — past 730; — to 731

Rabbi 449
raincoat 528
raining, it is 772
rare (meat) 321
raspberry 414
rate: one-half — 716; what is the — 260

razor 636; — blades 637
ready 613
receipt 708
recommend 296, 431
record (phonograph) 551
red 567
regards 27
regular 697
rent 216
repair 102, 654
reservation 246
reserved 169
restaurant 296
RESTAURANT, AT THE p. 24
RESTAURANT, AT THE (Conversation) p. 32
rice 403
right (direction) 141
road 221
roll (film) 611
room 248; double — 250; — number 283; — service 264; single — 249; waiting — 170
rouge 634

Salad 329
salesgirl 512
salesman 513
salt 343
sandwich 299
sanitary napkin 638
sardine 381
Saturday 750
sauce 350
sausage 382
say, how do you 63
school 153
scrambled 363
sculpture 458
seasick, I feel 182
seat 474; orchestra — 475
second 165
section: business — 132; residential — 133
sedative 639
see 28, 261
send 265, 715
SENDING A TELE-GRAM p. 56
September 760
serve 300
service 335; (religious) 453
seven 773
seventeen 773

seventy 773
sew 653
shade (color) 557
shampoo 640, 661
shave 660
shaving: — cream 642; — lotion 641
sherry 291
ship v. 511
shirt 649
shoe 102; — store 584
shoelace 530
shoemaker 583
shoeshine 666
SHOPPING p. 39
shopping, go 498
SHOPPING LIST p. 40
short 658
show v. 225, 459; (= tell) 132
shower 256
shrimp 383
side 147
SIGHTSEEING p. 35
sign v. 709
silver 544
silverware 552
simple 314
sink n. 257
sir 709
sister 12
sit down 25
six 773
sixteen 773
sixty 773
size 506
skating 518
skirt 531
sleep 680
sleeper (train) 196
slipper 532
slowly, more 54
smaller 504
smoke v. 198
smoking car 197
snapshot, take a 614
so so 22
soap 276
socks 533
soft-boiled 359
sole (fish) 432
some 605
something 501
son 10
soon: as — as possible 285
sorry, I am 49
soup 366

week 744
welcome, you are 69
well *adj.* 24; *adv.* 477; —
  done (meat) 323
west 140
what 81; — do you wish
  88; — is that 62
when 83
where 84
while, a 124
white 568
who 80; — is it 270

why 82
width 509
wife 7
will you 233
window 193, 304
wine 293; — list 307
winter 767
wish 5
with 5
within 720
without 339
woman 77

word 61
write down 60

Yellow 569
yes 64
yesterday 740
you 19
YOURSELF **p. 3**

Zipper 654